A N T

123 South Broad Street, Mankato, MN 56001, USA

Printed in Italy

Art Director: Rita Marshall

Book Design: Stephanie Blumenthal

Text Adapted and Edited from the French language by Kitty Benedict

Library of Congress Cataloging-in-Publication Data

Benedict, Kitty.

Ant/written by Andrienne Soutter-Perrot; adapted for the American reader by Kitty Benedict; illustrated by Monique Felix.

Translation of: La Fourmilière.

Summary: Discusses the wood ant's life cycle, nest, feeding habits, enemies, and benefits to humanity.

ISBN 1-56846-044-9

1. Formica exsectoides—Life cycles—Juvenile literature. 2. Formica exsectoides—Nests—Juvenile literature.

[1. Ants.] I. Soutter-Perrot, Andrienne. II. Title.

QL568.F7B4313 1992

595.79'6--dc20 92-15122

WRITTEN BY

ANDRIENNE SOUTTER-PERROT

ILLUSTRATED BY

MONIQUE FELIX

CREATIVE EDITIONS

WHAT IS AN ANTHILL?

In the mountain woodlands of Europe, the ground is covered with a carpet of needles, dead leaves, and twigs.

Sometimes you may find a spot where all this debris seems to have been cleared into a pile.

This pile is shaped like a cone with a rounded top. Its sides slope like a roof, allowing the sun to warm it and the rain to roll off it.

Close up, you can see many small holes, with little reddish brown insects scurrying in and out of them.

The mound can be up to three or even four feet high. Beneath it are tunnels dug equally deep underground.

This is an anthill. It was built by wood ants and serves as their nest. Of course, there are other kinds of ants that build other kinds of anthills.

HOW ARE ANTHILLS BUILT?

Wood ants usually build their nests on or around the rotten wood of old tree stumps.

The ants are clever builders. They use twigs and small branches to hold up the ceilings of the anthill's chambers.

The bottom chambers are the coolest. In them, the ants' tiny white eggs are stored.

When the eggs hatch into larvae, worker ants carry them to warmer rooms toward the top of the nest.

The larvae in the sunnier rooms develop into female ants, while those in the shadier chambers become male ants.

If it gets too hot inside the anthill, the ants make extra holes in the walls. They close them up at night or when it rains.

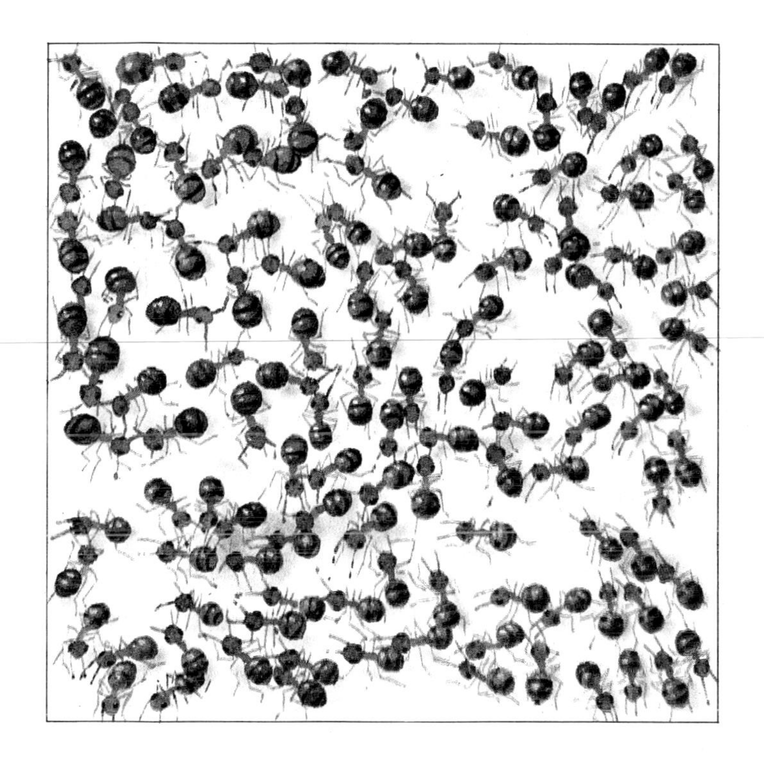

HOW DO WOOD ANTS LIVE?

Several thousand ants live in a wood ant colony. Most of them are female worker ants. They are called worker ants because they are very active.

The queen ant is the only female who lays eggs. She lays up to one hundred eggs a day throughout her entire life. The queen can live up to twenty years. Worker ants live only four to five years, or less.

Out of these eggs the larvae hatch. After they grow for a time, they become pupae, weaving silken cases around themselves. Inside, they change into adult ants.

The eggs, larvae, and pupae together are called the brood. The youngest worker ants tend the brood in ant nurseries.

Older workers are in charge of building, cleaning, and repairing the colony. The most mature ants are gatherers, going out into the woods to collect food.

The ants use their pincers to cut through the hard body parts of other insects. Then they eat the soft, liquid insides. Ants also like sweet foods, such as ripe fruit.

Some ants "milk" aphids, much as we milk cows. Aphids are tiny, nectar-sucking bugs. When the ants stroke their backs, the aphids release a sweet, honeylike juice that the ants lick up.

When they find a good food source, the gatherers store a great amount of food in a sort of pouch called a crop. Then they return to the colony.

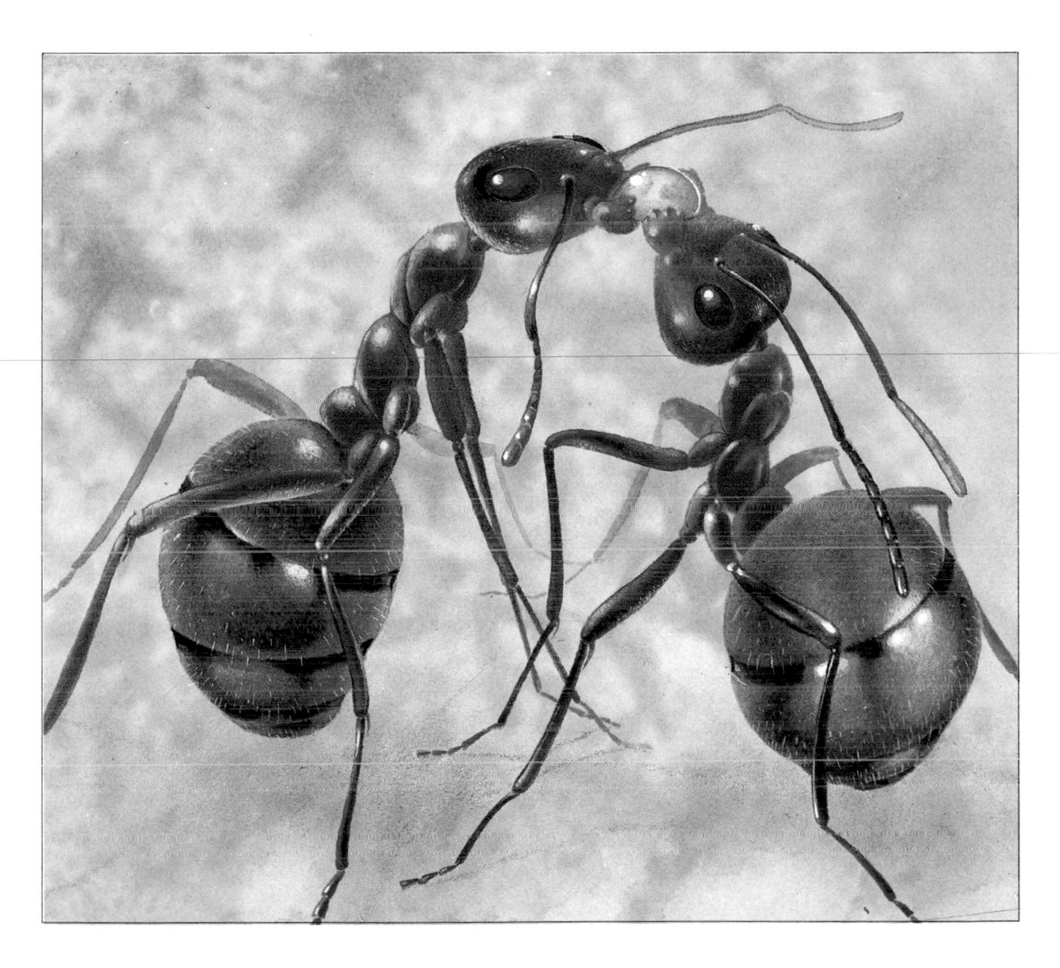

In the nest, the food is shared with the hungry workers. The gatherers keep only a little food for themselves. In this way, a single gatherer can feed many worker ants.

HOW DO WOOD ANTS HELP US?

During the winter the ants are much less active. The colony stays together in the center of the nest. The walls of the anthill are frozen solid.

Woodpeckers may bore holes into the frozen anthill. With their long tongues, they extract large numbers of worker ants stiff from the cold.

The anthill faces other dangers as well. Insects and ants of other species may invade the colony to steal the eggs and young. Hikers may make a game of wrecking the skillfully built nest.

We should remember that ants play a useful role in the forest. For one thing, they destroy large numbers of insects that do damage to trees.

In their constant to-and-fro motion, ants clean up the soil and move seeds that are sometimes much larger and heavier than they are. These seeds will germinate where the ants leave them.

Aphids that are "milked" by ants produce greater amounts of honeydew. The aphids leave this sweet syrup on leaves and branches. Bees then harvest it and turn it into real honey.

A healthy forest is home to many hardworking ants.

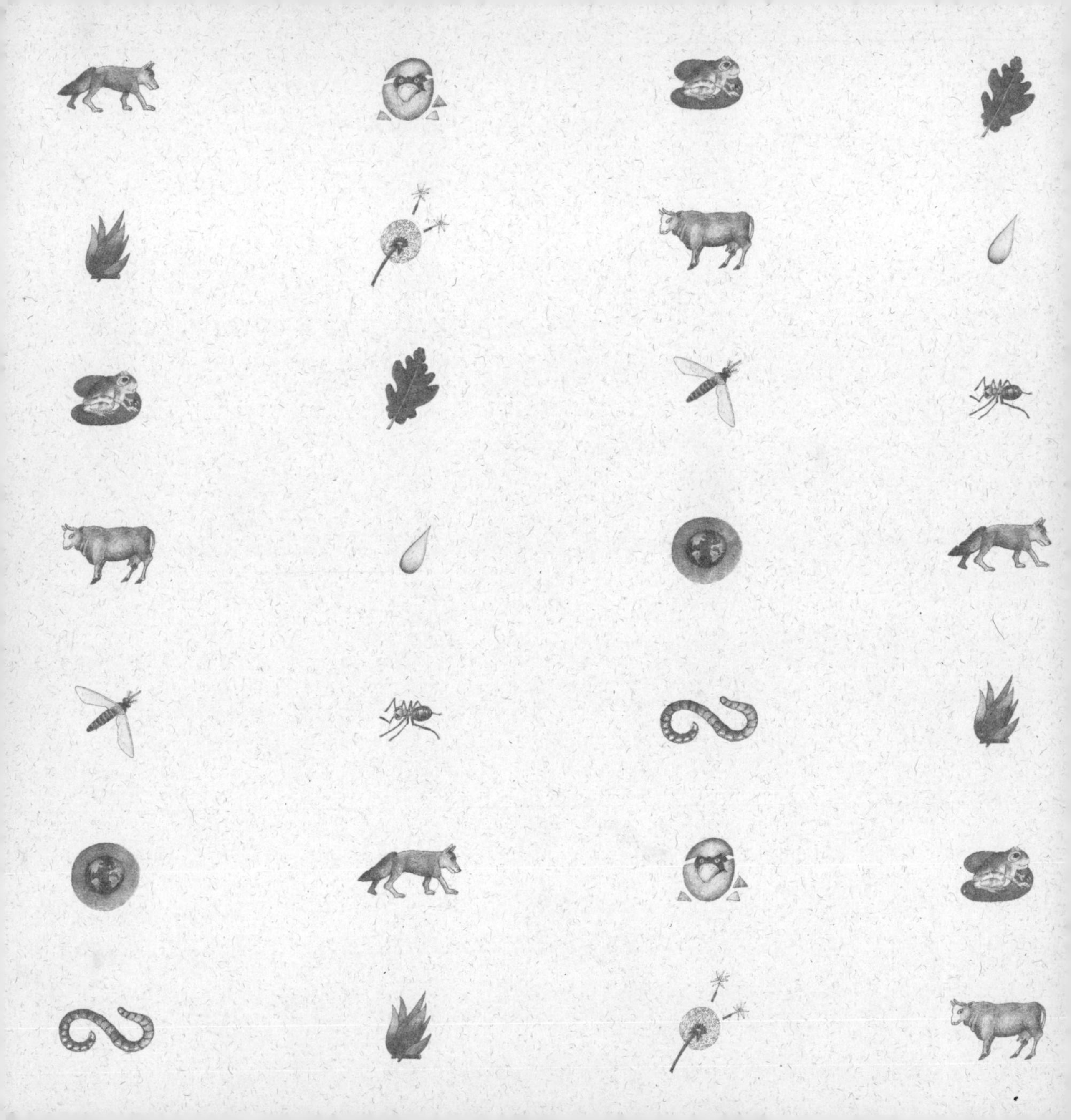